FROM BROKE TO BILLIONAIRE

How 5 Australians Became Billionaires

NHAN NGUYEN

GREEN MINT PROJECTS

A publication of:

Green Mint Projects Pty Ltd

as Trustee for the Green Mint Trust

PO Box 797, Lutwyche Qld 4030

Copyright © 2014 Nhan Nguyen.

This book is not intended to provide personal legal, financial or investment advice. The authors and publisher specifically disclaim any liability, loss or risk that is incurred as a result of the use and application of any content of this work.

National Library of Australia Cataloguing-in-Publication entry

Nguyen, Nhan, author

From Broke to Billionaire : how 5 Australians became billionaires / Nhan Nguyen.

ISBN: 978-0-9924841-0-1 (paperback)

Subjects: Finance, Personal--Australia.

         Wealth--Australia.

         Success--Attitudes.

332.02400994

Cover design: NGirlDesign

Typesetting/Editing: Power of Words

All rights reserved. Application for the copyright holder's written permission to reproduce any part of this publication should be addressed to the publisher.

CONTENTS

PREFACE	i
Why Did I Choose to Study Billionaires?	ii
INTRODUCTION	1
Which Traits are Common in Billionaires?	1
Which Sector for Wealth?	2
Which Ways can you Crack the Big Time?	3
What Systems Form the Basis of Wealth Building?	4
What do Billionaires do with their Money?	5
How do the Wealthy Invest?	5
1. GERRY HARVEY	7
Profile	7
Early Life	8
A Real Character	9
Business Methods	10
Giving Young Stars a Start	11
Investing Mix	11
2. COURAGE	13
Succeeding in a Crowded Market	14
Embrace the Limelight	14
Personal Selling	16
3. HARRY TRIGUBOFF A.O.	17
Profile	17
Early Life	18
Heart of Gold	18
Business Methods	19
Times have Changed	19
Future Vision	20
Lessons Learned	20

On Investing	21

4. VISION — 23
- Securing a New Income — 24
- Divide and Conquer — 25
- Think of Yourself as an Entrepreneur — 26
- Networking Your Way to Success — 28
- From Little Things, Big Things Grow — 29

5. FRANK LOWY — 31
- Profile — 31
- Early Life — 32
- Business Methods — 33
- Character Traits — 34
- On Investing — 35

6. PERSISTENCE — 37
- A Challenge that Would Deter Most... — 38
- A Strong Start-up Takes Persistence — 39
- People Make the Difference — 40
- Applying Persistence in a Strategic Way — 40
- Magazines for "Start Up" Entrepreneurs — 42

7. CLIVE PALMER — 43
- Profile — 43
- Early Life — 44
- (Business) Methods to his Madness — 45
- Character Traits — 46
- Litigious to a Fault — 46
- Into the Future — 47

8. BEING BOLD — 49
- Stepping into the Lion's Den — 50
- Ask and Ye Shall Receive — 51
- Boldness in the Service of Others — 52

9. KERRY STOKES — 55
    Profile — 55
    Early Life — 56
    Business Methods — 57
    Great People Behind the Wealth — 58
    Challenges to Fortune — 59

10. FINDING A MENTOR — 61
    Who Could a Mentor be? — 62
    How do you Attract a Mentor? — 63
    How can a Mentor Help you to Create Wealth? — 64

11. MAHA SINNATHAMBY — 67
    1. Make One Idea Your Life — 69
    2. Arise, Awake and Stop Not Till the Goal is Reached — 70
    3. Work Relentlessly — 71
    4. Be Fearless – Face the Brutes! — 72
    5. The Darkest Night Brings the Brightest Dawn — 73
    6. Pure in Thought, Word and Deed — 75
    7. Character is Established through a Thousand Stumbles — 76
    8. Everyone is Great in their own Place — 78
    9. Create your own Destiny — 79
    10. All Power is Within You — 82

CONCLUSION — 85
REFERENCES — 87
ABOUT NHAN NGUYEN — 91

www.BroketoBillionaireBook.com

PREFACE

Throughout all my years of studying wealth creation, pouring through thousands of personal development books, audio CDs, instructional DVDs, and so many seminars you couldn't imagine, I've been on the hunt for the "secret of success". While what I found was mainly theoretical, and I learnt much more from the school of hard knocks and losing cold hard cash, I did appreciate what the authors of these books and programs were saying.

The more I studied this information, the more I found that APPLICATION made the information relevant, not just the INFORMATION by itself. Ideas are great, insights are great, but without ACTION, information is dormant... and ultimately useless. I have a saying: "Too Much Information Gives You Constipation!"

Please enjoy this book, make notes, and get excited about what's possible for you... but rather than just reading to the end and putting it away, I urge you to take action as you read this book. Use the ideas given within to get started on things you may have been putting off, like:

- Start that new business you've been wanting to start
- Close the business you know that's way past it's due date
- Buy / Sell that property that you've been wanting to buy/sell
- Source the funding for your next deal
- Finish that unfinished project that's been dragging on and on.

This book itself has been a project that I've been wanting to do for a few years now... and now here it is.

Why Did I Choose to Study Billionaires?

Billionaires are the epitome of what our society defines as "ultimate success", i.e. having so much money you don't know how to spend it all.

Even though billionaires do enjoy a monetary and material success, it's more the incredible challenges they have had to overcome that makes them virtually "bulletproof". It's this ability to rebound from failures, and continually reach for the stars that inspires me about billionaires.

Sometimes we wait expectantly for someone close to us to encourage our dreams or acknowledge our talent, and this holds us back. I've learned that stepping through the fear, bolstering a belief in yourself, and never, ever giving up is the only way to make your goals become a reality.

May this book be part of your journey to whatever you define as "success"... and a life well lived.

Nhan Nguyen

INTRODUCTION

Which Traits are Common in Billionaires?

Top performers always seem to achieve the topmost results in wealth, and this is true in every field. In my study of Billionaires, I found that high intelligence or innate talent were not strictly factors for wealth—although some talent helps!

Class, status, beauty, higher education, or lucky breaks all seem to have little to do with success at the highest levels for the self-made entrepreneur. An above average inner drive is what all these people have in common. In many cases, a difficult upbringing seems to contribute to a lifelong hunger for success.

You will observe how the individual's hard work over many decades provides the momentum, and having a focus on building assets in a growth industry provides the leverage. Becoming ultra-wealthy is like creating a ball that rolls down a giant hill and keeps going over all obstacles.

Character traits are not the be-all and end-all though, with many of our Billionaires finding a mentor or partner who taught them how to be the best in business. An early stage partner often provided complementary skills and sometimes people networks that helped projects get off the ground.

Which Sector for Wealth?

As for sectors, property has been the greatest source of wealth for Australia's millionaires and billionaires. You'll notice the names of shopping mall developers and residential apartment developers in this book. Retail business is next largest, with investments ranking third.

Often these entrepreneurs don't start with assets in property, but they soon realise that cash doesn't grow by itself, and with inflation it devalues over time. Property, on the other hand, with or without the leverage from a loan, can greatly enhance the cash's power to grow, compound, and even pay off the bank funding in its entirety over time. So property is the vehicle of choice for many to create one's wealth and/or hold one's wealth.

> *"The median wealth of adult Australians stands at $US219,505 ($233,504) - the highest level in the world"*[1]
> - Credit Suisse Global Wealth Report 2013

According to CapGemini and RBC Wealth Management's World Wealth Report 2013, there are now 103,000 ultra high net worth individuals, referred to as 'UHNWIs' (pronounced 'unwees' not 'unwise') among us globally.[2]

To rank as an UHNWI, you need at least US$30 million in investable assets. Australia boasts 2,059 UHNWIs.[1]

Lower down the tree, high net worth individuals (HNWIs) are defined as those with US$1 million or more in investable assets. If you lived in the United States, Japan or Germany, you'd rub shoulders with more HNWIs, with 3.73 million in the US alone, and growing. Australia ranks 9th in HNWI numbers, with our long list of remarkable property and business entrepreneurs.

Although Ultra's number less than 1 percent of the global HNWI population, they control 35 percent of the total HNWI wealth. That's a whole lot of power.

"Wealth is not how much money you have, wealth is what you're left with when you lose all your money".
– Roger Hamilton, Wealth Dynamics *(Your Life Your Legacy audiobook, 2006)*

Which Ways can you Crack the Big Time?

We've all heard the stories of start-up Internet entrepreneurs who now make millions per year. In reality, property and mining has made a lot more high net worth individuals in Australia over the past 20 years, while the Internet ecommerce boom has spawned only a few multimillionaires and no billionaires.

However, having only been around for 20 years, ecommerce hasn't had much time to produce the multiplier effect. You see, it often takes a whole generation (around 50 years) for a family's wealth to really build. For a homegrown example, Kerry Packer grew a giant media empire out of a smaller newspaper business passed down from his father, and now James Packer has sold out of media and uses his early 'business training' to build on that wealth with flashy casinos.

Many Australians start in business with a professional service. Professional services includes businesses such as lawyers, management consultants, architects, town planners, engineering consultants, accountants, recruitment consultants, human resource management consultants, market researchers, PR consultants, events managers and many more.

These small or micro businesses contribute 76 percent of Australia's GDP, so their contribution is important.

Yet despite the talent and skill inherent in a specialist business, there are few professional services CEOs who have made a billion dollars from it. One of the reasons is that professional services have a limit: *time*. Rending these services, these individuals only have a maximum 40-60 hours per week to "make money" and charge clients their "hourly rate". Even at $200 per hour, there is a financial limit here.

Through leverage of OPM (Other People's Money) and OPT (Other People's Time), wealth accumulates. One professional services company founder who has cracked the billion dollar mark is financial services firm Platinum Asset Management's founder, Kerr Neilson. Through managing (other people's) money well, he's built his wealth to $2.4 billion. Observe though, that this service does not bill by the hour, instead it is a performance-based commission.

What Systems Form the Basis of Wealth Building?

Most billionaires in this book were completely focussed on perfecting their business, re-capitalising the business, and spending a small portion of the profits in their early to middle business years. At later stages, their business system had to change as the founder prepared for 'taking themselves out of the picture'.

There are different systems to get to the happy point where the founder is no longer needed to drive growth — but they do anyway. Every few years, a multi-empire builder like Kerry Stokes will acquire a new company that adds more assets and more income to his base companies. A single-empire builder whose focus was on one name and one system, Frank Lowy now protects the Lowy wealth by divesting parts of the retail fund, privatising and diversifying the assets in a family trust.

When a billionaire diverts from their usual sector and system, this can prove a financial mistake, unless they have an experienced partner in that arena.

What do Billionaires do with their Money?

Most billionaires tend to give around five to ten percent of their income away to charitable or political causes close to their heart. Billionaires already have enough money to grow their business or enjoy their ideal lifestyle, however, some are far more interested in giving to a cause than others. Gerry Harvey is one who does not consider it his thing to give 'handouts', but he does offer good opportunities to young performers in Harvey Norman's workforce.

Clive Palmer supports political causes, and changed the face of state politics with his $500 million donation to the failing National Party (now LNP).

How do the Wealthy Invest?

While many of us in regular jobs believes it takes high risk investing to gain wealth, millionaires globally tend to the conservative, putting nearly 30 percent of their wealth into cash and deposits. Probably because Aussies have witnessed more wealth built through property ownership, slightly more Australian UHNWI's favour property (as an investment) than billionaires around the world, with 10 percent of their assets in it.

Contrary to popular belief, the billionaires surveyed do not take on high-risk strategies; many of them learned to stick to their particular field. They all started small, sometimes with a partner to help, and brought their ideas and enthusiasm to new deals.

With the leverage of many activities and compounding returns over decades, these hard-working individuals looked up one day and realised that they were billionaires. Not one of them decided to retire to a beach, even though most of them could have lived off their growing wealth by about age 55. Many are now in their 80s and still "going to work".

1

GERRY HARVEY

Estimated Net Worth: $1,440,000,000

"It should be compulsory for every wealthy bloke—anyone who has $5 million—to spend 10 per cent of it owning racehorses, otherwise the money gets taken off you" [3] – *Gerry Harvey.*

Profile

Gerry Harvey portrays his identity as the 'lovable larrikin from Western Sydney', all the while gathering a national retail and property empire.

With friend Ian Norman, Gerry started a small auction house and then began Norman Ross in 1962, becoming successful chain store owners and millionaires. In 1982, Grace Bros bought Norman Ross. Within 3 weeks of acquisition, Alan Bond convinced Grace Bros. to sell it to him. Soon thereafter Alan Bond got rid of Gerry and Ian. Upon management failure, Gerry and Ian started Harvey Norman all over again. Gradually the company once more became a retailing giant and a large landlord. Gerry and his second wife, Katie Page, manage it in tandem. Ian Norman is a board member.

Gerry also has a love of racehorses and was co-owner of Magic Millions, a leading racehorse auction, for ten years. He doesn't believe in giving to charity, but he is a big believer of simple living and being rewarded for good work.

Early Life

Born in rural NSW in 1939, Gerry grew up on a farm. He liked to work during the holidays, and really wanted to be a farmer. The family was unable to afford agricultural college, so Gerry, thinking he would become an Accountant, decided on a Commerce degree.

After two miserable years of failing subjects, he left after seeing an ad in the paper that promised 30 quid a week. That was the motivation he needed, even though he never saw himself in sales. It involved selling vacuum cleaners door to door, and only 1 in 100 people employed survived in that job, as he admits himself.[4]

After struggling on for a bit, Gerry decided to learn from the best salesmen in the company... what did they do? He just wanted to be as good as them. He ended up being their no.1 salesman, and then he moved on to selling TVs. Ian Norman also sold vacuum cleaners and became a close friend.

People often wonder what it takes to get started on the road to success. Everyone has to start somewhere, building on success, and Gerry Harvey was no different. Gerry and Ian agreed to start a furniture and electrical auction room (selling mainly secondhand furniture, but sometimes ducks and bric-a-brac) in an old building in Arncliffe. Gerry advertised and went out to people and offered them a fair price for the furniture—if they waited a month for the cash. So he would get the furniture and then auction it at the store and give them the cash, less a profit.

Because they worked very hard, seven days a week, turning over a lot of stock, the business soon grew. It was Gerry's idea to turn half of the auction house into an electrical and furniture showroom.

Having enjoyed small-time success, Gerry and Ian went into partnership with Keith Lord in a Norman Ross store in Neutral Bay, borrowing up to their limit. A short time later Keith wanted out, so Gerry and Ian bought the store on finance.

A Real Character

Gerry Harvey is a real contradiction in terms. His office in Homebush West is fairly plain; his rural home unpretentious, he spends little on clothing and lunches, and poo-poos highly paid executives. Yet he holds a huge portfolio of retail shares (earning himself $1 million+ annually just from dividends), owns two horse stud farms and other property, and has many decades of good credit standing.

While other billionaires may seem like outsiders, Gerry is welcomed at all levels of society. He hobnobs with the key players in politics, media and retailing, but then he gets a "cheers" by patrons when entering a Pub (Harvey Norman sponsors the National Rugby League).

Another contradiction is in his vision for selling computers to ordinary Australians. Gerry took a punt on opening computer superstores in the late '80s, but he is the only top executive in Australia who doesn't use a computer daily!

Business Methods

"Go Harvey Norman, Go!" is the familiar cry on radio ads. While Harvey Norman is worth $3 Billion, for decades Gerry has had a studio next to his office to record his own radio advertisements (which are simple, direct and sales-focussed).

Not for him the advertising gurus or the upmarket business advisors. Gerry relies on himself and the opinion of his second wife, Katie Page, herself a savvy businesswoman who is CEO at Harvey Norman.

Being super-confident in promoting his wares, Gerry still sells the Harvey Norman brand even after 50 years of retailing. He takes any opportunity to talk with the media, and was an early vocal opponent of online ecommerce. This confidence likely stems from his success in sales; even though he admits "I didn't show anything that would make me a salesman. I just watched others and thought, I could do that"[4].

Gerry often uses his powerful brand to get the upper hand in Joint Ventures. Gerry did a JV deal with Ossia Group, held 60/40 between Harvey Norman and Ossia. The company owns 11 Singapore shops, and even though the name would not be recognised there, Harvey Norman is the name on the stores.

He will never back down from a fight. One battle was with Compaq, who planned on opening stores in direct competition with Harvey Norman. He threatened—and then did—withdraw Compaq computers from Harvey Norman shelves, thus costing Compaq a $97 million account.[4]

Giving Young Stars a Start

From his early experience, Gerry knows it's far easier to learn from someone who is good at sales than to battle on your own. He is passionate about rewarding people based on performance. Unique to the industry, Gerry offers a department franchise to 'star' sales staff for no fee. That is, if the trainee can prove he or she would succeed in running the store. He also started a Graduate program and finds successful role models inside the empire for the proprietors-in-training. Gerry has said:

> *"Businesses are made by people. We've proven time and time again that you can have wonderful shop, and put a bloke in there who's no good, and he'll stuff it up. Put a good bloke in, and it just turns around like that."*[5]

By tying their income to their store's profit, Gerry ensures that franchisees are motivated to perform well.

Investing Mix

A curious mix of shares, horse studs, retail stores and property makes up this retailer's assets. Harvey Norman's asset base is ~$4.27 billion, inclusive of a property portfolio valued at ~$2.14 billion.

Because each property is firmly in the hands of Harvey Norman, they became a super-landlord. They earn revenue on leases, as well as sit on capital gains from the large retail buildings built on cheap land.

Gerry's next grand plan is to build office and residential developments on Harvey Norman-owned sites, with the first right on top of the Domayne store in North Ryde.

Some of the other assets Gerry personally invests in are: Rebel Sport shares, also a subsidiary of Harvey Norman, 200 broad mare horses, horse farms, and property on the Gold Coast.³

Gerry's primary income is tied to results, so if his business does well, then his share dividends pay well. If retailing is down, such as in the past three years, then his income is also down.

2

COURAGE

"Develop success from failures. Discouragement and failure are two of the surest stepping stones to success." – Dale Carnegie

---

People such as Gerry Harvey just seem to have the fire and confidence needed to sell, don't they? It seems crazy then that he says he wasn't a 'born' salesman... just like anyone else, he had to learn how to sell and promote products. It takes both courage and passion to do this.

Gerry is forthright, and his no-holds-barred advertising attracts people to Harvey Norman stores. He tries to identify with us as middle class, "one of us", despite the fact that he's a billionaire—and we in middle Australia are not. This persona helps him keep on connecting to customers.

While other brands mimic competitors, resulting in a faceless and soulless company, those in the right wealth-creating flow try to be themselves to the nth degree.

In this chapter we're going to learn that selling is a key factor of success, and selling yourself is not egocentric.

Succeeding in a Crowded Market

Let's examine the reason that Harvey Norman has succeeded in Australian retail where WOW Sight & Sound, Retravision, and Kleenmaid have all failed. These retailers have suffered from internal fraud or mismanagement and falling store sales (with stiff competition from online stores). So what keeps the Harvey assets profitable?

It could well be the maturity of the man behind the company. Gerry holds back from the madding crowd, such as when tech stocks took off in 1999 or when forming property trusts was the thing to do. But when he sees good value for his company, he pounces to grab a bargain from a failing major retailer.

He also has the courage to expand his empire in a single leap, such as when he made a takeover bid for $51 million to purchase Rebel Sport. He takes a long-term vision to build new wealth-producing assets, even if it's met with general skepticism.

> *"Work ethic, people skills, the ability to promote people and the ability to delegate"*[3] are key factors to success (Gerry Harvey).

Embrace the Limelight

If you've spent many years in your field, think about all the insider secrets you know that will save people future heartache. You need to get your message out there and start attracting some great opportunities that align to your key values. But how?

Many of us are not accustomed to promoting ourselves, and certainly our voice in the media is minor compared to Gerry Harvey, so what easy things can we do to attract and embrace the limelight?

You can start by building your personal profile and reputation, such as:

- Offering insights through blogging to a particular market, or writing a book
- Doing deals with higher-level partners
- Joining an industry association or national networking group
- Speaking engagements at clubs, chambers, meetups, etc.

Presenting at a University or local Chamber of Commerce can be a good first step towards speaking at a large conference, seminar or trade expo. For both name recognition and connection building, speaking to a professional audience is second to none.

For those who want wealth for a charitable mission, you'll need to be able to engage an audience by putting forth big goals and personal insights. There are many stories about people who have had no money, yet spoke passionately about a vision they had and thus attracted the needed investment in a worthwhile enterprise.

Journalists don't only want famous people to quote these days; they're also looking for people who are leaders in their niche, in order to get a comment or a profile story. This is your chance to get your message out to a wider audience. To encourage more media interaction, have a media kit: a factual bio (biography) and clear photograph, as well as clippings of any published stories, available on your website.

You could also join a network or industry association with national coverage and subscribe to "call outs" for experts (that come from various media).

Personal Selling

"80 percent of your success as a salesperson will be determined by your attitude and only 20 percent by your aptitude."[7] - Brian Tracy

While successful at what they do, a lot of businesspeople have a fear of selling and of being told "no". Yet selling is based on a process of building rapport and trust, i.e. having a good interaction with people. Then you go on to enthusiastically divulge your knowledge of the product and encourage the prospect to buy or commit. If you've done the rest of it well, then the "asking for the commitment" part of the process will be natural and easy.

To be successful, the salesperson must have certainty that the solution is right for the buyer. This is because certainty—or lack of it—always comes through in body language and speech. I'm sure you have encountered an uncertain salesperson who couldn't explain the features of a product, much less name three benefits.

I'm sure you'll agree that when you get more practice at something, it becomes natural—you get better at it. It's the same whether speaking to an audience or one-on-one personal selling: the more you do it, the easier it becomes. So get practising!

Recommended: *"Advanced Selling Strategies"* or *"Closing the Sale"* book or audiobook, by Brian Tracy, author of 300 books or audios on selling, management, and principles of success.

3

HARRY TRIGUBOFF A.O.,
A.K.A. "High Rise Harry"

Estimated Net Worth: $4,950,000,000

"Australia's population may grow to maybe 55 million... I'd like to see 100 million, because I believe we will have many things to do here besides drilling holes and selling coal."[8] *– Harry Triguboff*

Profile

Founder and Director of *The Meriton Group*, Harry Oscar Triguboff has overseen the construction of almost 60,000 residential apartments in Sydney, Brisbane and the Gold Coast.

He has won many awards for his contributions to the Australian property industry over a span of 50 years. A humanitarian, Harry has also given millions for youth education in Australia and also opened an institute that helps Jews find their identity in Israel.

Early Life

Harry Triguboff was born in Darien, China on 3 March 1933. He spent his early childhood in the Russian community of Tientsin (now Tianjin), south of Beijing. This has no doubt helped him forge a connection to the Chinese, who were early individual buyers of his apartments.

Escaping from China during the Lenin years with his parents, Harry first came to Australia in 1948 and was educated at Scots College in Sydney before attending Leeds University (UK). He got a degree in textile engineering and began his working life in textile businesses in Israel and South Africa, but decided to return to Australia in 1960.

Harry Triguboff became an Australian citizen in 1961. A hard worker, he eventually owned a taxi service and a milk run. After getting some experience finishing his own house, he organised to build his first block of apartments with a partner in 1963. His second project, a block of eight apartments near Sydney Airport, led Harry to establish Meriton in 1968.

Even though his plans almost got derailed in a market slump in 1974, Harry got a crucial 30-apartment approval through and went on to become Australia's most successful residential property developer.[10]

Heart of Gold

Harry Triguboff is a long-time philanthropist, providing millions of dollars each year in financial support to many causes. He has received two honourary doctorates and many other honours and awards, including an Officer of the Order of Australia.

In 2011, Harry won the Gold Harold Humanitarian Award for supporting charities that educate youths about drugs and wellbeing. He also established a centre in Israel that focuses on immigrants and Judaism.

Business Methods

Harry Triguboff was one of the first Aussie developers to see the potential of apartment living, at a time when most people desired a suburban block.

Known as "High Rise Harry", he certainly lives up to his name. Meriton recently developed the 81-level, 262m high, Infinity block in Brisbane, and also built Sydney's highest residential apartments, World Tower.

While these are at the higher end, earlier residential blocks in the '70s and '80s were much less luxurious. Harry built his business through building apartments at the affordable end of the scale. He attracted many Chinese buyers with urban apartments that maximised space. He also made it easier for buyers to get housing loans in hard times.

Over the past 50 years, Meriton has grown to become Australia's largest apartment builder. In the recent downturn, Meriton have capitalised by building modern serviced apartments in Sydney, Brisbane and the Gold Coast on undervalued land, then adding resort style facilities.

Times have Changed

Thirty to forty years ago, people did not admire his buildings—in fact, he was criticised for building huge concrete apartment blocks, 'the slums of the future'.

These days, with less affordable housing close to city centres and a growing urban lifestyle demand, apartment living has become acceptable, even alluring. So now Australians buy around half of Meriton's residential apartments. Serviced apartments in the Gold Coast, Sydney and Brisbane have also become an excellent money tree for Harry.

Fifty years ago when he laid all his savings on the line, Harry could never have foreseen all the changes in the Australian housing landscape. When he first started, people in Australia had little money for putting into real estate. Now they understand its capacity for growth.

Future Vision

His vision for Australia is to become a population of 100 million people—maybe that's why he often builds some towers so big! He sees western Europeans who are bitter at their recent economic woes as the next wave of immigrants.

Still growing his business even at 80, Harry has recently bought a $100 million development site near Sydney Airport, and says he is "still capable, health wise and brain wise".[9]

Lessons Learned

Back in the 1960s, Meriton was caught in a credit crunch and the ANZ Bank threatened to close Harry down. Ever since then, he has vowed to never be beholden to banks again. He said recently "on the building side there is no debt. But there might be in the future. Debt doesn't frighten me"[9].

There is no debt because Meriton has usually relied on cash reserves rather than financing in order to grow. It seems to have paid off, since last financial year Meriton took $1.2 Billion in revenue from residential apartment sales and management of serviced apartments.[10]

Harry likes to keep a close eye on each development as it's progressing. This is why his developments are often within an hour's drive of his office. Harry's foray into building apartments in South-East Queensland began after he and his wife bought a penthouse on the Gold Coast. Harry says his weekly visits give him a "real feel for how the developments are progressing rather than just reading someone else's reports in the office".[11]

On Investing

1. Stick to the Formula that Works:

Although he has considered other types of development and business opportunities, he told BRW, "I would never diversify for the sake of diversification. I would only diversify if I found something better than apartments, but I never found it—so I didn't do it."[9]

2. Create Multiple Sources of Income:

One of the clever things that Harry has done is set up Multiple Sources of Income, often referred to as "M.S.I." Out of the 55,000 dwellings that Meriton has developed over time, approximately 3,000 dwellings are held at any one time. These collect rental income, a continuous source of passive income that comes in whether or not Meriton builds another building ever again.

IMAGINE HAVING 3,000 RENTAL PROPERTIES PRODUCING $400 PER WEEK, EVERY WEEK, FOR THE REST OF YOUR LIFE… THAT'S $1,200,000 PER WEEK PASSIVE INCOME…

3. Defy Markets by Becoming your own Bank:

Another clever way that Meriton defies the market downturns, as well as financing constraints, is by offering "Vendor Finance". To understand this basically, let's look at a simple example on a $400,000 property:

Buyer has a 5% deposit and good income, but lending may be tight, and so banks will not lend them the funds required to purchase the property outright at $400,000 sale price. Meriton still wants a deal to be done, so offers the buyer the opportunity to purchase the property and they will "finance" the property at say 6% p.a. interest over 25 years.

It's a good deal for the the buyer... they can get into a property with no bank funding, plus it's a good deal for Meriton... they get ongoing income from a genuine buyer who would have otherwise not been able to purchase a property from them.

4
VISION

"A goal is not always meant to be reached, it often serves simply as something to aim at." – Bruce Lee

---

When we look at Harry Triguboff's successful business life, we can see that his 1960s/70s vision was to provide cheaper modern apartments within the city bounds. This, along with his tough, hands-on approach, helped to build his present fortune. Yet it was a vision well ahead of its time, just as today he sees Australia growing and attracting a large population.

While others would have been crying about the demise of the quarter acre and the impact of high rise housing, Harry just ignored the cacophony and kept on expanding. Secure in the knowledge of what potential buyers wanted, and with an eye for detail and costs, Harry never let his ego or his fear take over.

This kind of future vision is also based on real movements in the market. Ten years ago, Meriton identified an opportunity in the market for luxury, self-contained, apartment sized accommodation for short stays. The Group consulted with leading global hotel groups and then formed a new brand, Meriton Serviced Apartments. If Harry and his management had feared stepping out of their comfort zone, then a new gap in the market would have been missed.

So, how can you expand your vision... and earn extra income?

Finding the Treasures in your own Life

> *"The trick to finding your treasure involves opening your eyes, and opening your heart. Look in front of you, and within you. Some of you are afraid to look because you have grown comfortable struggling with troubles you've come to expect.*
>
> *Believe me when I tell you that you have been given everything (for happiness) you need.*
>
> *Everyone is good at something, and you'll come to find out that the more you share your treasures, the shinier they get, and the more valuable they become. We can become rich beyond imagination when we discover that we are all sparkling jewels."*[12]
>
> – Silas Harper, finder of real diamonds in his previously 'worthless' farm.

Securing a New Income

Let's see how expanding your vision works in a specific situation with a fictional person. Say Anna notices in her area that there is a University but a lack of good student accommodation. Unfortunately Anna doesn't have the lending power for flats or a 5-bedroom house, so she decides to make some spare income by converting a downstairs space into a granny flat. She gets all the estimates on the property renovation and it seems feasible.

Her accountant lets her know that she has to declare the taxable income, but any costs incurred for a tenant's electricity, water bills, and maintenance on that part of the house is deductible against that income.

This means it can get complicated if Anna goes to sell. That portion of the house that was rented (or housed a home office) will not be wholly tax-free, as it is if she retained her principal place of residence Capital Gains Tax exemption. Often though, Capital Gains Tax is not as much as we think it will be, since it is just a portion of the profit gained from sale, based on our taxable income rate.

Despite the drawbacks, the income over time can put you well ahead, giving you a definite return on the investment in your property. In Anna's situation, a probable cash flow of $200 per week, less $30 expenses for a 48-week letting period per year, gives $8,160 p.a. – less initial costs.

It would be wise for Anna to plan for that extra income to either reduce mortgage debt or be diverted to a starter investment account. That way the tenancy is making a noticeable difference to her wealth.

Divide and Conquer

Have you looked around your suburb and noticed more small developments popping up? Are rental vacancies in your area really low (1-2%)? Then you could capitalise on an increasing need for townhouses, duplexes and other subdivision developments.

Let's take David as an example. He owns a house on a large section (850 sqm, allowable for subdivision) with room for a driveway up one side to the rear where there's plenty of room. After ten years, he has a manageable low mortgage, so it could be possible to build another house on the block and then divide the Titles before sale of the new section (or divide then build and sell).

Before David does this though, he'll want to ensure profitability. It's advisable to get an independent valuation of the property development by certified and experienced Valuers, and find out possible Development Application costs. This is called a "Feasibility Study" and you could opt to get a property strategist to help with this.

If you think you could subdivide your block, the first step is to find out about DAs and Easements from Council. They will let you know the basic rules in your zone.

You may need a mortgage broker to help judge your ability to lend for building in stages 'on site' (ensure you add in any spouse's income). Plan for a maximum amount that is 10% over the cost estimates. You wouldn't want to extend up to your original loan limit and then have a sudden cost blow-out, meaning all work stops.

What other ways can we use our imagination and current market needs to create income?

Think of Yourself as an Entrepreneur

Australians that have lived through the 1980s might think of entrepreneurs as an Alan Bond type, a huge risk-taker. Yet if you want to start a profitable enterprise that grows and grows, you need to start thinking of yourself in a new way.

Anyone who thinks up a new idea and takes it to market is an entrepreneur. It doesn't necessarily mean you have to lend large amounts of capital. Sometimes taking small steps to a larger goal works equally as well.

Opportunities abound; it's just a matter of picking one that is right for you. Some of the things that contribute to making someone a successful entrepreneur are:

- Identifying personal strengths and leveraging them in the right way
- Defining your target market and spotting specific opportunities
- Learning about marketing and sales strategies
- Creating your own business brand and identity
- Developing a financial and business plan
- Persistence!

Catching onto a trend for eco-friendly products, some women have created cheap and trendy totes to cart your shopping in, as they didn't like carrying those clumsy fabric supermarket bags. Sascha Griffin, founder of 'Pinklily', got started by filling a need for home delivery of clear shoe-boxes and other hard-to-find products for women.

"If you are going to own your own business or be great at what you do—passion, commitment and time is imperative"[13] – Sascha Griffin

If you don't have an idea yet, why not assist people in your neighbourhood to recycle their unwanted clothes? If you're handy with a needle, you can fix small problems or make items more on trend. Helping keep good clothes in circulation is good for the world. Pick out items that would sell well online, and give clothes a 'back story' (people love stories, even on eBay). Any leftover clothes can be donated to local Op shops.

Networking Your Way to Success

A structure like Network Marketing/MLM means that the profits are distributed through the tiers of marketers (agents). Often criticised for rewarding the top performers, people forget that this distribution is also how traditional business operates. Like any other business, the executives and CEO make 20 times the profits of the bottom tier of workers.

In a multi-level direct sales system, anyone with the right people skills and motivation can usually move up to a higher income, 'executive' tier. As direct sales marketing companies are set up to allow entry-level owners to gain a share of the income pie, the marketer's income results are directly related to their efforts.

The keys things to look for in a MLM opportunity are:

- Products are something you see the value in, even without reward. Some systems dictate you pay $3,000 to $5,000 up-front for video products, but you don't earn until you get two others to pay that price. The quality of the products is crucial to the longevity and popularity of the whole system.
- Great sales training and personal development support.
- An unsaturated market in your locale. If you've had two or three offers of demonstrations, then that enterprise probably has too many distributors already in your area.

Network marketing is a great training ground for business thinking and self-development. The most successful people in this industry, not surprisingly, are also the most resilient and persistent... so in Chapter 6, the trait of persistence is our focus.

From Little Things, Big Things Grow

If you're a Mum or Dad with young ones and a penchant for baking, then baking for market stalls and parties is a good trial step to a larger retail business. It allows you to try different recipes and see which sell the best, without the worry of expensive retail space.

Other steps to entrepreneurship might involve: going to a workshop about property options, doing a property renovation course, attending network marketing training, or simply studying the masters in your industry... how did they get started?

This type of activity can get you thinking more like an Entrepreneur... someone who is brimming with original or creative ideas.

From Broke to Billionaire

5

FRANK LOWY

Estimated Net Worth: $6,800,000,000

"Never give up! People don't understand how persistent you have to be. You come up against an obstacle and you have to find a way of moving forward. You take detours, navigate between the obstacles and make it happen. Unless you are very strong and convinced you can succeed, you will be swept away."[14]
– *Frank Lowy*

Profile

Frank Lowy's start in life could not have been tougher; he had to make money as a kid, and as a Jew, evade capture by the Nazis.

Frank fled Israel and migrated to Australia, meeting fellow ex-Hungarian John Saunders. Lowy and Saunders brought the high-density shopping mall concept to Australia, starting in Blacktown, and then in the 1970s exported the improved concept back to the Americans. Lowy's focus was to systematically build the shopping malls to provide good yields.

Now aged 83, as Westfield Group chairman, Frank has amassed a $6.87 billion personal fortune. Lowy's three sons (Peter, Steven & David) are also CEOs or Executives in Westfield Group, and will continue growing the Lowy empire in a more private way.

Frank also has a passion for football. He is current Chairman of Football Federation of Australia, bringing his vision to help create an A-League.

Early Life

Frank Lowy was born in 1930 in Czechoslovakia to a Jewish family. His father was mainly a travelling salesman and his mother had a small grocery store for a few years. His dad was terrible with money and wasted the marriage dowry.

Anti-semitism was rife during the late 1930s and the Lowy family's life was made much harder. Many Jewish people including some of their relatives were deported. The Lowys moved to Budapest and sold the house and shop. As his father couldn't get work, Frank and his siblings had to make a living (he was 11 then). In March 1944 the Nazis invaded Hungary, and sadly Frank's dad was captured. Although Frank looked for him for days, he was never to be seen again.

Even though he was the youngest of four children, Frank could sense the dangers, twice moving his mother to hide from the Nazis. Escaping with his brother, and leaving his mother in a safer part of Budapest, Frank went to work and study in a Palestine Youth Settlement. At just 17, he fought with the Jewish Army in the Israeli War of Independence for around two years.

He migrated to Australia from Palestine with his brother in 1951. He got a storeman job, then started working in a sandwich shop. After meeting his wife Shirley at his soccer club, Frank took his 'dream job' as a delivery driver, where he earned many times the average wage by being hard-working and fast.

Frank Lowy was a young man when he started working for John Saunders. Frank impressed the Hungarian immigrant, as he went about helping John's delicatessen make deliveries, always on time. So they went into business together, first with a coffee shop and then in shops and small housing developments.

John was also a refugee from WWII Jewish persecution. Together they put their joint savings to start their first coffee shop to join John's migrant deli in 1955. Finding the cafe time-consuming, the pair took to building small-scale housing and then shops.

They made their first real estate profit by subdividing a vacant lot. The partners' first well-planned shopping centre complexes were small (14 stores) by today's mega mall standards.[15]

Business Methods

Early on, Frank learned how to build malls to make maximum use from the space, and this is what made Westfield Group much more yield than the usual American spacious malls.

Being both fresh to Australia, John and Frank innovated in the novelties of migrant deli foods and espresso coffee.

Westfield expanded nationally in NSW and Queensland and forged links with retailer GJ Coles. The group moved from being a developer to a mall owner. Often coming up against problems with council planning, purchasing and so, on, Frank had to forge on tirelessly. In 1977 Westfield took their techniques to the US, with modest-sized multi-level malls.

Even though John Saunders and Frank Lowy made great business partners in the establishing years, eventually that became strained. John was edged out as Frank, then based in the US, re-structured Westfield financially and also brought his three sons into the business. John left the business in 1986.

When Frank tried his hand at buying and running Channel Ten, the effort quite quickly lost money, as he had no experience in negotiating in this market. Even though he could have left it insolvent, Frank put $200 million back into the TV Network and re-focussed on his core business, shopping centre ownership.[15]

Character Traits

Frank Lowy's world revolves around his philosophy of "never give up" and making maximum effort, as failure is not an option for him. Failure used to mean death or at least hunger for him, and so he carried this inner drive through his life.

Meticulous detail work, particularly with finance, has been another of Frank's key attributes. His ability to plan down to the letter made a good counterpart to John Saunders' more entrepreneurial, instinctual style.

Working long, stressful hours to the point of strain and fatigue was common as Frank's fear of failure drove him, even once Westfield was a huge success. He often cancelled holidays and almost never talked about personal issues with those outside the family.

On Investing

As Chairman of Westfield, Frank Lowy is Australia's wealthiest property developer and second wealthiest person overall. Property, in fact, has created more millionaires than any other industry, including mining, with 54 of BRW's 200 richest gaining wealth mainly from property.

Westfield's share price increased 300 times since listing in 1960, so being a shareholder (with 21 per cent stake) just in retail property was lucrative enough for four decades.[16]

It seems that the Lowy family agreed to gradually diversify away from retail and privatise their wealth. In 1998 the Lowy family sold a $400 million equity stake in Westfield Retail, and in February 2013 the Lowy Family Group sold their full 7% stake in Westfield Retail Trust (for $663.7 million), bringing their private group assets to around $3 billion.[17]

From Broke to Billionaire

6
PERSISTENCE

"The most important lessons I've learned from my experiences in athletics haven't been physical ones... they've been about personal qualities like dedication and determination, perseverance and persistence, goal setting and achievement, and most of all, an unshakeable sense of optimism and self-confidence."[18]
– Jane Flemming, gold medal Olympian in Heptathalon

———————————————

As both Jane and Frank point out, being persistent and having the confidence to break through barriers is key to success in any endeavour. People who sit around making excuses for themselves are not the same people taking the podium or becoming chairman of a large company.

But why is it so tough to be persistent?

In this day of Internet noise and mobile communication, many of us suffer from never-ending distraction. Because of the constant flow of income-producing ideas and new solutions, the 'bright, shiny object syndrome' is apparent among many younger entrepreneurs.

This lack of focus makes it very difficult to achieve anything. A steady focus on one goal and consistent effort is needed in most endeavours, but especially in building wealth through business. Even though some of these new opportunities and technologies could prove advantageous, you must not let new projects take you off your true path, the one where your values, goals, expertise and talents all align.

A Challenge that Would Deter Most...

You don't hear very much in the news about successful female entrepreneurs who started from scratch. Karen Corban, co-founder of Universal Events (now Universal Stars), has been running personal development and wealth events in Australia for 20 years and has a net worth of around $8.3 million.

Karen started at just 21 years old with successful clothing boutiques, but she decided she wanted to help others learn how to apply NLP.[19] Karen, her co-founder Ken Wood, and their team have now touched the lives of half a million people. On her way, she helped start *ThinkBig!*, a personal success magazine.

When Karen got on the phone in the mid-1990s to promote tickets to events, she says it was "very challenging" because the field of Neuro-Linguistic Programming was unknown in Australia, and people were somewhat afraid of personal transformation. Australians are more accepting these days; more people believe that personal change can mean a new level of success.[20]

Can you imagine getting on the phone and calling people to ask them to try something new, to take a weekend off and come and hear a speaker? How about filling a 500-seat auditorium? It certainly takes courage and persistence to succeed in business, and a strong belief in the value of what you're doing.

A Strong Start-up Takes Persistence

You might have heard of novel ideas that use modern online technology or mobile apps. These are called "startups", and behind every startup is a fired-up entrepreneur.

Startups normally need venture capital to employ technical developers and invest in some marketing. Rather than bank loans, startups tend to use these three models to get funding: angel investors, seed funding and crowdfunding.

Angel investors are cashed-up business owners who want to see a new idea and person succeed. Besides a good return, many want input into the business.

Seed funding is where a group of venture capitalists (perhaps through a competition) offers genius tech startups a sizeable amount and expert mentoring, often in exchange for an equity share.

Crowdfunding is done on a website, where a fledgling enterprise offers various levels of buy-in memberships to anyone, e.g. donate $20 to get a branded key ring and a silver membership to the site. Suits artists, authors, community groups, and product inventors. (See **www.Kickstarter.com**).

According to a Harvard paper, first-time entrepreneurs only have an 18-22% chance of succeeding, whereas a 'venture-capital-backed entrepreneur' who succeeds with one company has a 34% chance of succeeding in his next capital-backed venture. So for the new startup entrepreneur, it would be beneficial to start out as a partner or mentoree to a successful entrepreneur.[21]

People Make the Difference

It seems to be quite easy these days to find collaborators, but it's really tough to keep on going past financing knockbacks, website dramas, finding customers, finding good suppliers, and so on. It's been said that a startup or small business makes or breaks on "the people".

Of course, there are online communities where you can meet the people who can help you technically or creatively launch a new venture, e.g. www.cofounderslab.com; www.techcofounder.com; www.startmate.com.au.

It's not just others' skills you are looking for; it's temperament. What does your personality bring to business? A creator, the type who usually comes up with many ideas, would be best to join up with a pragmatic person, someone who thinks of the finance, the company structure, and where continual revenue is coming from. Add in a supporter, someone who is good at organising details and providing help for everyone, and you have a well-rounded team. Everyone playing to their stregnths may just make the project work!

Applying Persistence in a Strategic Way

Creating a great business that grows exponentially is also about finding a market that is growing by 10, 20, or 30 per cent per year, according to Richard Koch.[22]

Even if you don't know exactly the growth numbers, it's fairly easy to tell that retail bookstores are declining (bye-bye Borders) and eBooks are steadily growing in sales. Around 30% of all Amazon books sold are electronic books.

If you doggedly persist in your desire to, say, sell books in retail stores, or offer 10-12% commission-based recruitment services to corporations, you might see the odd company whizz past your business to success. (For example, RecruitLoop, which found a new pay-for-what-you-get model in recruitment).

In this fast-changing world, persistence in working in a maturing or dying market is shortsighted. One day you will look up and say, "who moved my cheese?" (in other words, "who cut my income?"), as the analogy goes in the insightful book of the same name.

So the moral is to have the personal trait of persistence and apply it to the right model of business, one that is in growth phase. Stop looking for the magic formula to riches! You don't need the talent or smarts that you think you do, to succeed.

In fact, Geoff Colvin's research found that greatness doesn't stem from talent and DNA but from practice and perseverance. He remarks in a 2006 article, "The best people in any field are those who devote the most hours to what the researchers call 'deliberate practice.' It's activity that's explicitly intended to improve performance, that reaches for objectives just beyond one's level of competence, provides feedback on results and involves high levels of repetition." (Read more in Colvin's book, *"Talent is Over-rated"*).[23]

You can apply this to business, Colvin says, by setting a new intention with daily tasks. Instead of just setting out to get a task done, you aim to get better and better at it.

Magazines for "Start Up" Entrepreneurs

'*Entrepreneur*' (US) has a Startup online article bank and business plans. http://www.entrepreneur.com/startingabusiness/index.html

'*Startup Smart*' (Australian) has 5,000 free articles online, including about crowdfunding. www.startupsmart.com.au

'*Blueprint Entrepreneur*'... a small digital magazine available in iPad's Newstand. Hacks, technology, and expert tips for the online entrepreneur.

7
CLIVE PALMER

Estimated Net Worth $900,000,000

"I never worry about money because if you live your life properly, you always have enough money to do what you want to do. Only my wife counts the money, I just count the experience; we're all travellers through life."[24]
– Clive Palmer, 2013

Profile

Included due to his wealth 'magnetism' and media and political profile, Queenslander Clive Palmer is a one of a kind.

After a 'no boundaries', globe-trotting upbringing, Clive started off in law, was disillusioned and then moved on to making a fortune in selling land and then buying and developing lots.

After many years building the commercial research company ACRD, Clive Palmer saw the potential in mining... setting up Mineralogy Pty Ltd.

He also owns Waratah Coal, Queensland Nickel, Palmer Coolum Resort on the Sunshine Coast, Palmer Sea Reef Golf Course at Port Douglas, and two other golf courses at Robina, Gold Coast.

Clive Palmer kept his association with conservative political parties over the years, and was once the Media Director for the National Party in Queensland. He now holds Federal senate seats under his own 'Palmer United Party'. Clive also owned the Gold Coast United Football Club from 2008 to 2012.

Early Life

Born in Melbourne in 1954, Clive Palmer was the youngest of two in a tight-knit family headed by George Palmer. Growing up, Clive suffered from bad asthma attacks. Seeking a better and warmer environ, Clive's family moved from the sleepy town of Williamstown, Melbourne to the vibrant Gold Coast.

George Palmer was himself an entrepreneur, creating a successful coach lines and tourism business. Circling the world many times with his family, George saw the world as his oyster. Besides adventure, Clive also learned from his father how to use the media to promote his projects and demonstrate their importance to the community. (George himself promoted his own film when just 16).

While Clive started off flat broke, and admittedly, quite lazy while at university, he soon found his voice and became a paid student lawyer for the PDO (precursor to Legal Aid). He spoke out against corrupt police tactics that he observed in murder trials and was swiftly demoted.

Clive, still just a youngster, was disappointed with the Queensland Labor government and justice itself, so he left the world of law. He eventually got a job as a real estate salesman for a land reseller who became his long-time friend, Ian Ferguson.

Such was Clive's talent for communicating, friend Harry Fong joked early on, "... you can either be a lawyer or a self-made millionaire".[25]

The young entrepreneur went on to set up his own property development company. By buying land and apartments at under market value, holding then selling, Clive reports to have had $40 million in assets by age 29.

(Business) Methods to his Madness

Clive's business methods might be hard to discern for the casual observer, distracted by his dinosaur theme park and plans to recreate a mighty ship with Titanic II.

It's true that his outlandish statements and grandiose vision get Clive many Press pages. But steadfast determination to achieve his vision and the ability to convince others to broadcast his vision, is what got Clive where he is today. For instance, Clive got State ministers and a Queensland Premier to officially support his research commercialisation venture, ACRD.

After sitting on his lucrative un-mined magnetite lot for 20 years, his Mineralogy business finally got cash flow. For over 20 years, Clive worked at getting a large and wealthy partner to buy the magnetite deposits, with one trip to Russia and two to China. The eventual deal with the Chinese backer added hundreds of millions to his bottom line in one fell swoop.

"He's ahead of his time on many things, and people don't understand that" – Clive Mensink (nephew).[25]

Clive Palmer seems to always come up smelling of roses.

Character Traits

Clive never acts as if he might have to squirrel or save. Every year he gives generously to political parties and selected charities. In 2008, Clive rescued the broke Queensland Liberals with enough to keep them going, donated $400,000 to the Nationals, and also took over support of the Gold Coast United Football club, enabling them to get into the A League.

To jibes at his influence in politics, he jokes that he doesn't need to donate to be in their pockets, because he "already makes more than they do, and has better jets and a better helicopter."[25]

He even donated generously to a JFK memorial because he was supportive of the family; in fact, Clive "mistakenly gave them more than they asked for".[25] His money often follows his beliefs.

Clive also shows generosity to those loyal to him. In 2010, he gave 50 Mercedes Benz B-Class sedans to his mining employees as a Christmas bonus. He also gave all 750 of his long-time workers a holiday trip to Fiji. The bonuses cost him about $10 million altogether.

Litigious to a Fault

Clive has been in court many times because he'll follow anything up that he feels is not right. He sued the universities who breached contracts. He sued the Commonwealth over ACRD agreement breaches, and he even sued the ANZ Bank for $500 million. All this litigation—settled quietly out of court—led to the end of ACRD.

Clive also lost a large sum in a failed attempt to build a huge Steel Mill in Newcastle, but the State Government lost more. Clive decided to drop the case for compensation.

Into the Future

Although the mining magnate was riding high at $2-3 billion wealth in 2008-10, the recent slowdown in iron ore, and mining generally, has led to his estimated wealth going under the $1 billion mark. Yet it really doesn't matter to Clive and has not affected how he spends or allocates his money. His grand vision for Australian society is what drives him on, and he's had that enthusiasm all his life.

After a lot of campaigning, Clive Palmer won three seats in the Senate in the 2013 Federal election under his own Palmer United Party. Once again, he beat the odds and pushed his way through.

The China First Project, selling coal to China over a ten-year period (valued at $7 billion in total), is also slowly moving forward. Approval to Waratah Coal for a new mine in Queensland's Galilee Basin has been granted, however, coal export prices are presently low.[26]

From Broke to Billionaire

8

BEING BOLD

"Whatever you can do, or dream you can, begin it! Boldness has genius, magic, and power in it."
– Johann Wolfgang von Goethe

Have you ever met someone who was amazingly confident and you just wanted to go along with them, swept up in their tide of enthusiasm? Even before the wealth came, Clive Palmer was this type of person. For example, when selling land lots, he used to walk over and shout from the other side of the paddock so buyers could see how large it was.

Clive has certainly not met with any less challenge than ordinary folk, but he has taken on those challenges with a bravado one can only admire. Would you have been bold enough to grab and pay for an unproven mining lease the week it expired, with nary an investor or a digger to realise the yield? This one decision led—a full 20 years and many negotiations later—to one wealthy windfall.

Stepping into the Lion's Den

Long-time business investor, Richard Koch, has made millions from boldly backing businesses. He doesn't look for the 90 percent of businesses who will stay small; he looks for businesses who are leaders (or could be leaders) in a niche, where that niche is experiencing upwards growth of 20 percent+ per year, and he invests in them. He also helps with strategy if they only have a small team.

At times the businesses, like a new way to broker bets on an online exchange, were met with suspicion by the usual venture capitalists. Richard saw BetFair as a company that aligned to his 'star principles'. Betfair was launched in June 2000, becoming the largest betting exchange in the world, and "spitting off cash".[27] (Read more in *"The Star Principle"*, 2010).

When you're new and green, just boldly leaping into something new is not the answer either. Because of a lack of rungs on the board, you're blind to the obstacles; perhaps you optimistically think every good idea will work in reality.

That's where stepping into the lion's den 'holding the hand' of someone wiser is going to help. Popping up around the country are 'experts who teach'; people who have blazed the trail with success in:

- Building a low-cost, high-tech business
- Making profits from property development
- Making a passive income from residential property investment
- Buying and developing a passive income online business.

Stepping into a bold new venture is a whole lot easier when you're with someone who has done it before. The learning curve is steeper, and the price paid up-front is often less than the costs of getting bitten by the unknown factors. We talk about this more in *Chapter 10: Finding a Mentor*.

Ask and Ye Shall Receive

It seems the antithesis of what society teaches us about self-sufficiency, but have you tried asking for what you need? Just like the quote above denoted, there is a providence that comes into play when one is bold enough to broadcast exactly what one wants.

Say you're starting up a new business and you need new customers. Focused on setting up your marketing to an audience, you may forget that the best source of new leads is people you know... people who already trust you. I'll illustrate this point with two types of business starters.

The 'paying advertiser', Jim, assumes his friends are not in the market for his service. He focuses on the cold sell and pays for leads. Jim finds it really tough going until he has his first few satisfied customers.

The 'networker', Cassandra, who thinks laterally, tells everyone (whether a supplier or a friend or another owner) excitedly and succinctly how she is going to get results for a certain type of client. This means that everyone who trusts her is carrying around a certain image in their minds, waiting for the time when they talk to someone else who has that problem. Having 10 or 20 people keeping you in mind is sure to spark a few new leads and interest.

Sure, the business networker still needs a professional identity. But a business card or brochure can then be a reminder of that "problem solving" option, rather than something to give anyone in business.

Boldness in the Service of Others

Commitment to a cause is something that charity founders often have before they ever boldly ask for, and receive, what they really want. But where does this desire to step up come from? In some, boldness to act stems from the shock of seeing others living so far below their own basic living standards.

From the glamour and culture of club promoter in New York City, Scott Harrison questioned his shallow life. He turned to volunteering as a ship photojournalist into West Africa. This "Mercy Ships" mission into Liberia meant he saw first hand that people were in dire need of both better medical help and access to water.

An inner drive to ensure clean water for better health led Scott to found 'Charity: water'. That charity is now world renown and has many others behind its force.

> *"For me, charity is practical. It's sometimes easy, more often inconvenient, but always necessary. It's the ability to use one's position of influence, relative wealth and power to affect lives for the better."*
> – Scott Harrison.

You'll notice that Scott believes that channeling good from a position of wealth and power can truly improve people's lives.

Far from our arcane impression of the wealthy hoarding away their money or spending it mainly on luxuries, the truth is, many of Australia's wealthiest people are also the most generous. For instance, Graham Tuckwell recently made the largest-ever Australian donation (of $50 million) to a University, the ANU, to fund a scholarship program.

In others, it's an act of courage that leads to a better life for cancer sufferers. Concerned about his sister, actor Samuel Johnson recently unicycled around Australia to promote breast cancer awareness and research. Sam used his position of fame and influence to raise money and improve lives. And there are a thousand more stories just like this one.

So if you have a belief that you cannot be good, kind *and* prosperous... it's time to replace that belief with a new one! It's difficult to make those first steps, putting your principles and reputation on the line, but once you do back your beliefs and boldly go after a goal... there will be no stopping you.

From Broke to Billionaire

9

KERRY STOKES

Net Worth: approx. $2,400,000,000

"I have a fear of public speaking. It's very hard work. Words are not my skill and because they're not my skill, I have to work doubly hard".[28]
– Kerry Stokes

Profile

Now 73, Kerry Stokes is a fascinating enigma. His business success and connections with others in business are a stark contrast to his earlier, troubled private life.

With the income from property speculation in Perth and his own Real Estate agency, Kerry made a start on his empire in the late 1960s. After shopping mall deals and other developments came off, Kerry and a partner moved into buying West Australian regional television network, South West Telecasters, in 1975. He acquired a Canberra TV network and newspaper, and in 1995, the Seven commercial TV network and other media outlets.[29]

Kerry has a passion for Australian artefacts and art, yet business remains his main muse.

With Seven Group Holdings owning WesTrac Group, an earth-moving equipment dealer, this exposure to mining has provided Kerry's empire with 'rich' diversification. He has many other business interests in online media, petroleum, hire equipment, and property.

Early Life

Born John Patrick Alford, Kerry was adopted as an infant by Matthew and Irene Stokes, who lived in poverty in Melbourne. He was, says one biographer, a little neglected by his poor adoptive parents. Kerry said himself they gave him "little emotional input".[30] He never knew his real father's name, and his mother had died sometime during his childhood. He also had trouble with reading and writing as he was unable to keep words in his mind.

Generally speaking, if you received little nurturing as a child, then you barely know how to give it yourself. Certainly with his first marriages and children, Kerry did not seem to cope well—leaving when things got tough.

Kerry Stokes left school at 14 to work hard as a shearing hand. In his teens he worked for an electronics factory, ran some races in the local Athletics Club, and (after losing their address and then re-finding them again) began to support his adoptive parents. He bought them a house in Western Australia and continued to lend support until their deaths.

After marrying Dorothy Ebert and doing varying jobs, Kerry settled into a real estate agency in Perth and traded in property as well. That was just the start of new possibilities for Kerry in the world of business—a place where he excelled.

Business Methods

The public think of Kerry Stokes as mainly Channel 7's controller, but this is just part of the Seven Group Holdings' media pie. In fact, Seven West Media is now Australia's largest diversified media business and includes 50% ownership of Yahoo!7 online.[31]

Kerry has a great knack to spot a business opportunity at the perfect time. He was really active in the 1990s Perth property boom (as a real estate agency founder), and more recently he spotted a mining equipment opportunity before the mining boom. Yet Kerry doesn't really have a passion for the type of business; it's more the untapped opportunity that he is after.

After an impressive run acquiring stations for their regional TV and radio network, Kerry and partner Jack came up trumps. They sold 'Golden West Network' through their corporation, BDC, to Northern Star Holdings for $206 million, ostensibly a loss. But Northern Star quickly had to sell GWN to satisfy existing media regulations, and guess what? Golden West Network was sold back to Kerry Stokes in December 1988 for $54 million.[29]

Then Kerry segued to a completely different industry, when he spotted that Bond's sinking empire meant the rights to sell Caterpillar heavy equipment in Western Australia was up for grabs. In 1988, Kerry took a stake in Morgan, the US company that owned the rights, before eventually buying the franchise itself.

The business became WesTrac. It grew quickly because Kerry bought rights to sell Caterpillar into China's growing northern provinces, as well as NSW. When the mining boom took off, so did WesTrac's value, although now it has dipped with the slowing down of the mining sector.

In around 2005, Kerry took control of the Seven Network and eventually, West Australian Newspapers. Cross-media ownership laws had been relaxed.

Kerry's knack for timing continued. Right before the GFC in 2006 he sold a 50 per cent stake in Seven Media Group to private equity firm Kohlberg Kravis Roberts for a whopping $3.3 billion.

BRW recently named Kerry Stokes its best Rich Lister of the past 30 years, not just because of his consistent placement on the list since 1984, but also due to his "wealth, power, influence and entrepreneurialism".[32]

Great People Behind the Wealth

In finding success, Kerry had Jack Bendat as a mentor and partner for 18 years. This partnership was perhaps the first of Kerry's successful joint ventures. Together they built 11 regional shopping centres and co-owned a Western Australian television network (Golden West) from the 1960s to the 1980s.[29]

Sometimes the apprentice outgrows the master, and that was true in this case. Kerry wanted to expand nationally, while Jack did not, so they parted as friends.

He also met other successful business types while partnering with Mr Bendat, like Competitive Foods Australia head, Jack Cowin. Mr Cowin has told BRW that Kerry Stokes "always surrounds himself with intelligent, loyal people, many of whom have worked for him since the early days".[29]

Kerry's heirs are Ryan and Bryant Stokes, sons of his second wife, Denise Bryant. (He is now married to wife number four, Christine Simpson). Ryan is CEO of Australian Capital Equity, while his mother has stepped down from the board. The two children of Kerry's first marriage are not spoken of these days; they are just regular citizens.

Challenges to Fortune

Expensive challenges are often the test of an entrepreneur's mettle. From 2002 to 2007, Seven spent $200 million in legal costs to try to testify against the main pay TV rivals, claiming that they killed off Seven's pay TV venture, C7. Actually one of the longest-running cases in Australia, the case was dubbed by journalists as "Kerry Stokes against the world".

Even the judge said the case was "extraordinarily wasteful". But during that time, an undeterred Kerry became a 21.5 percent shareholder in Consolidated Media Holdings.[28]

Luck and timing also played a part, as WesTrac's growth due to the mining boom and a recovery in Seven's earnings covered the losses from litigation. True to form, Kerry bounced back to make that grand $3.3 Billion deal. He also merged WesTrac with his media group to form the ASX-listed Seven Group Holdings, thus strengthening his empire and creating more wealth.

From Broke to Billionaire

10

FINDING A MENTOR

"I really admire Richard Branson, who proves that you can still have a lot of fun while building a market leader"[33]
– Gabby Leibovich (co-founder, CatchoftheDay.com.au)

———————————————

While many of us try to walk the lonely path in business or investing, there is real value in finding yourself a mentor: someone who has walked a mile in your shoes and now mentors or coaches a select few people. Role models are also helpful; people who display traits and attitudes you can model and whom provide an inspiration to you.

Kerry Stokes was lucky to meet someone who proved instrumental to his early success: Jack Bendat. While partnerships can often go wrong, in this case Kerry knew that he had met a partner who was a mature, practical businessman and ex-builder. And after all, Kerry was just an ambitious football player and real estate man when meeting Jack.

Together they formed public companies, built shopping centres, and

Jack helped to develop the notion of the shopping centre. Jack remembers the partnership "as one of the best in Australia".[34]

Who Could a Mentor be?

For Clive Palmer, an early mentor was his boss (and later, business friend) Ian Ferguson. But without first modelling all the positive aspects of his entrepreneur father George, who knows if his success would be the same?

So our Mum or Dad, or other elders, can also be our role models and mentors. Robert Kiyosaki's 'rich dad' mentor was instrumental to his success. Without the education provided by his friend's Dad... and reflecting how different it was to his own Dad's life theories, then Robert might have become someone else entirely. Maha Sinnathamby identified so clearly with Mahatma Gandhi that he was a strong role model, helping to shape Maha's life principles.

A mentor could also be a paid Business Mentor/Coach or Career Coach. This type will typically provide some education in your field of choice, and pepper it with real-life lessons and examples. You may have heard that 'the fastest route to success is through failure'... so if you can learn something from a mentor's failure or challenge, then you will speed up your own rate of learning.

Having a mentor or coach helps keep you focussed on your big picture, your strategy, rather than getting ground down by all the small hurdles. An ongoing mentor also keeps you accountable to your stated goals.

How do you Attract a Mentor?

"To initially entice the right Master to serve as your mentor, you will want to mix in a strong element of self-interest. You have something tangible and practical to offer them, in addition to youth and energy."[35]
– Robert Greene

You might think that a poor, homeless, young black man wouldn't have a lot to offer. But when a volunteer asked, "what are you missing at the shelter?" James Ward replied, "my time management is not working out". He mentioned his offer of a place at University but that he couldn't afford the tuition. The volunteer was Jessica Sutherland, a University alumna who also struggled with being homeless as a teen, and so she went out of her way to create a fundraising campaign. This created a ripple effect. People were attracted to the cause, spread the message, donated, and James got his first year's tuition paid. Off he went to University a very happy young man.

In many ways, honing your skills and striving for self-development is the right foundation for attracting a mentor. The blueprints provided by such figures as Gandhi, Nelson Mandela, Barack Obama, Oprah, Robert Kiyosaki, Anita Roddick, and many others, are freely available to read. Look for the traits and attitudes that set these idols apart.

It's also important to find a mentor related to your chosen field. For example, if you want to deliver healthy soup to the elderly on a mass scale, try to find someone who has been through a similar journey, perhaps with a different type of product. They can point out the hidden obstacles in getting to that market, and various paths around them.

How can a Mentor Help you to Create Wealth?

If you are still wondering if a mentor could help you... consider these real life stories:

> "I started out my property career researching property deals for Nhan back in 2003 and since then have been involved in putting together over **$200 million** of commercial and industrial property deals. Nhan pushed me to put my first offer on a property and as a friend and mentor over the years through my own ups and downs, has given me a lot of **valuable advice, ideas and opinions** for which I am grateful. I believe Nhan is a wealth of knowledge and grounded in his thinking, he is a long term player and most importantly has the results to prove that he is an authority when it comes to making money from property."
> – Richard Mulligan – Director, Rich Initiative Property Group

> "I'm a property investor and developer and also a friend and associate of Nhan Nguyen. Nhan and I met many years ago, and last year when I was having lunch with Nhan, we discussed joint venture deals. Nhan then instructed and mentored me on how to do joint ventures, which I am very grateful to him for. **I currently have two full-time joint venture partners and I also am finishing a deal that I made $50,000 on.** Not bad over a lunch deal with my good friend Nhan Nguyen."
> – Neale Kretschmann – Property Investor, Gerain Properties

Mentoring in this way means that the experienced mentor is the guide for the student's initial steps, and always strives to keep the novice on track for their stated goals. A good mentor will also link the novice up with trusted specialists and even project partners, if they come across a good fit.

Some of our Billionaires' early partners have also been mentors. Partnerships borne out of complementary strengths and skills are often the most effective, as long as everyone knows how to communicate effectively. A healthy respect of each person's skill-set and experience always goes a long way toward maintaining solid relationships.

Next we are going to explore the principles of a man who left his imprint on Brisbane's landscape, someone who definitely came from 'broke' and who is now very nearly a billionaire.

From Broke to Billionaire

11
MAHA SINNATHAMBY

Estimated Net Worth: $820,000,000

The Sinnathamby family mantra is: "I'm the best, I can do anything, I never give up" (Maha Sinnathamby)[36]

Creating the Right Conditions for Maximum Success

Mahalingam (Maha) Sinnathamby cannot claim that any advantage through birthright, family, race or nationality helped his biggest dreams to materialise. In fact they were more of a hindrance to success.

Born to a poor Malaysian family, this restless individual saw his father imprisoned during World War I. He endured lonely trips from school to his village hut twice a day, reading biographies on the way. But his father had grand plans for his eight children, and saved diligently to pay for six of them to go to university overseas.

Travelling to Sydney to go to University, Maha tried his best to follow the course his father had set him... to be an Engineer. But he could not get an engineering job in Australia, so rather than face unemployment, Maha made the best of it by working as a real estate agent. He made calls all day long, earning himself a dribble of commissions. Maha was then offered a 'real' engineering job.

While engineering was a good foundation, Maha longed to realise his dreams... and so he started a development partnership in Perth. He then ran into a great big wall when attempting to put all the company's buildings into a trust. It was the late 1980s and as interest rates climbed, he could not sell up (as the assets were frozen), nor could he pay his way out—as much as he wanted to. As investors pulled out of the capital raising, he was left with a debt of $42 million.[37]

Through the depths of despair, the phoenix rose again... Maha inspired Bob Sharpless to join his new team. When Maha spotted Opposum Creek, a vast tract of wooded forest and hilly dryness, with nary a service there, he envisaged something that the other twenty or so developers could not see. On the 2,860 hectares, he saw a master-planned city, including schools, shops, restaurants and parks. In his mind, he saw today's Springfield city.

Together Bob and Maha visited large master-planned communities around the world in order to plan their city. Even though Maha was laughed at and hindered by lack of capital and a lack of investors at a crucial stage, he kept on, always managing to scrape through with a win-win solution at the last hour.

So what conditions brought this man and his team to succeed, where all others would have given up? To explore this, we're going to look into Maha's ten principles for success from the book, *"Stop Not Till the Goal is Reached"* (Wiley, 2012).

Three core beliefs underscore the principles: *persistence, hard work* and *positivity*. Maha says he has lived these beliefs for the past thirty years.[37]

1. Make One Idea Your Life

A powerful influence on Maha's life, Mahatma Gandhi's one idea was 'social justice'... first in South Africa, and then India.

Maha's one idea for the past twenty-two years has been to create a thriving city where he could bring his passion for education to life. Indeed, Springfield has eight schools, colleges or further education facilities, including a large university campus.

Yet what brought this passion into life was not because Maha was an A-grade student, since he sometimes failed his engineering subjects. We could surmise it was the influence of his father's conviction that "good education leads to a better life". And with some university degrees offering 97 percent full-time employment rate for graduates and an above-average starting salary, there is some evidence to support his idea.

If you are currently lacking the direction for your 'one great idea', then Maha advises:

- Think about what 'definite major purpose' could be brought to life through your work. Dedicate yourself to just one big thing, not twenty so-so things.
- Make a start – action towards a goal brings other possibilities.
- Find others who also value the same overarching vision.

Summary.

If you want to create a legacy, this leaves no time to pursue several minor things. If you follow Maha's advice, you will dedicate yourself to one thing and master that area, as with mastery comes success.

2. Arise, Awake and Stop Not Till the Goal is Reached

It isn't the surroundings of the man that makes him successful; it is how he directs his life. First, of all Maha had a bold vision to complete, but even before this he knew the power of a vision of something greater.

Then there is the no minor matter of getting it done. Getting his University degree by day and driving taxis by night, Maha learned early on that it's necessary to manage your time very effectively.

Getting up at 4 am on a regular basis, Maha seems to have an incredible drive to achieve his greatest ambitions. But it is for a very valid reason that this 'arise early' principle came to be. Using the quietness of that time to reflect, Maha is able to come to a decision or plan a course of action without the usual distractions.

Many of us go around complaining how busy we are. Yet being busy is not the same as being productive. Maha ensures he is working on the right priority before starting each task, and then puts everything into getting as far as he can with it. Many noted teachers of prioritisation also say to start on the most important thing first and continue as far as possible before switching tasks.

Sometimes we need to sacrifice a little leisure time to achieve something outstanding. It is not because of amazing talent that makes a swimmer get up at 5am every morning to swim 100 laps of the pool; it is her dedication to her goal.

Is it time to take the leap? Follow the steps of Maha:

- Create a definite vision
- Rise early – this will allow time for meditation and planning

- Productively work towards your goal.

Summary.

How much time do you spend watching the news? How much time reading friends ramblings on Facebook? How much time do you really need to spend? If you can cut the time spent reading the media down to 5-6 minutes a day, then it leaves you plenty of time for self-education, true human connection, and business planning.

Combine this with an early start and proper planning, and the 'busyness excuse' melts away. Are you willing to get up early to achieve more of what you want?

3. Work Relentlessly

Napoleon Hill's definite major purpose was to learn the principles of success from America's top 100 most powerful men. It took him 25 years of research, interviews and experiences to do this, but imagine if he'd stopped after one year, thinking "well, I've surely done enough now to put together a book". No, because he was motivated to find the truth... and common principles behind the men's success, not just by earning a few small royalties, he worked on until his major goal was reached.

Working relentlessly is needed, and yet it is entirely pointless without the forces of the other nine principles.

Maha advises to put aside your fixed vision of the reward for hard work. For example, my focus in writing this book is to shine a spotlight on principles of the wealthy entrepreneur's success, not because I desire instant publishing renown. To have no expectations of a set outcome from your hard work is also to release yourself from self-made pressure, regret and disappointment.

If you just "put in the effort, carefully finetuning and altering as needed, then you will reach the goal set, and reward will come in the exact form of compensation that it deserves".

Maha works relentlessly, and if you want to take up this principle, then you must:

- **Pursue success, money will follow.** Inspiration comes in many forms, but accumulating cash isn't one of them.
- **Recognise that you can always do better.** Being the one who offers to do more, or learning more, or gaining more experience, will put you ahead of the pack.
- **Say 'yes' to it and work out the how later.** This means that you meet the fear of a risky, time-limited opportunity with optimism and faith.

Summary.

Once setting yourself a task, work tirelessly on it. Forget about what you are owed or what your result should be. Power on, knowing that the effect of your positive actions will take place at a later date.

4. Be Fearless - Face the Brutes!

Fear is probably governing your actions more than you realise. Do you front up to that person at work who always takes credit or just chalk it to experience? Do you avoid your partner when they have a gripe?

Sometimes, once you face a problem fearlessly and openly, you'll find it is actually much less troublesome than you thought.

Many often complain that their list of tasks is endless. Imagine if you had to write a development proposal so new and complex that it warranted an Act of Parliament. Imagine too that you must woo the Lord Mayor, the Deputy Premier and the Minister for Housing to your plans before it goes to approval. For Maha and Bob, the task of getting a huge master-planned city approved warranted a completely fearless and invigorated approach. Complaining would have been pointless.

The steps to instil this principle in your life are:

- **Burn your bridges** — commit to this course of action and cut off all other paths that could help you merely 'get by'.
- **Detach** — it helps to relax and take time out from a stressful situation.
- **Tirelessly seek solutions** — if you come clean and admit you really want to work out a way forward but cannot see how, often someone else will offer a solution or some help.

Summary.

If you stay committed to an idea and stay open to new solutions, then there will always be a way through. Having faith in yourself and your ideas is essential, and this confidence can win others to your way of thinking. People will also pick up that enthusiasm is your driver, not desperation.

5. The Darkest Night Brings the Brightest Dawn

> *"Life is difficult. This is a great truth, one of the greatest truths."*
> - M. Scott Peck

It's human nature to look upon a successful person and think, "how lucky she is" or how looks and talent must have been bestowed more lavishly on him or her than on you.

But life, as Maha and M. Scott Peck agree, is a never-ending series of obstacles that you must climb over, with problems to confront. While we must not operate based on a fear of people sticking pins in our plans, there is also great power in accepting that adversity will come... it's just a matter of when.

Seeing failure as black and white, you might believe that all failure is bad. Yet it is only the failure of giving up your dreams that is true failure; everything else is a temporary setback. It is important to see your difficulties, financial or otherwise, in an objective light and understand that your character or ability is not to blame.

How can you take steps to instigate this principle?

- **Ask everyone.** Have you contacted everyone in your network about your problem? What about outside advice? Don't stop until a satisfactory solution comes to light.

- **Manage the perceptions of others.** Because people only want to do business with those that are successful and confident, it is vital to manage the perceptions of outsiders.

- **Never, ever give up.** Failure is giving in to obstacles that overpower your spirit. If you choose to never give up, except when it makes good sense to, then you will never feel a failure.

Summary.

If we live in fear of failure and let it dampen our spirits, we will never fulfill our greatest dreams. At times we will have doubts, worries and obstacles, but if we portray to the world a confident, able front, then it will make it that much easier to get back on the right track. Someone else may even come up with a solution for you.

6. Pure in Thought, Word and Deed

Every manmade object, big or small, began as a thought, an intangible idea. That idea worked its way through spoken and written words, drawings, and was acted on (the deed) to become the object that you see.

Each element itself has its own power and must work together in harmony with the other two elements. Without adequate thought nor good communication to others, people on your team will have only a vague idea of the goals, so they will run around looking busy but being ineffective.

Yet when there is unity between thought, word and deed—with adequate energy spent on each—this inspired mission then takes on a life of its own. A balanced trilogy seems to attract the right investors, staff, and customers.

That doesn't mean that you won't have hostile enemies or those who misunderstand. Yet for the billionaires in this book, staying true to their initial vision, inspiring others to their vision, and carrying it out thoroughly, was enough to get difficult projects off the ground.

Even though many of us have read Napoleon Hill's *"Think and Grow Rich"*, we still don't realise that what thoughts we think and what words we use heavily influences our actions... and hence our results!

Emotion behind those thoughts causes a chain reaction... particularly if they are consistent and repeated. If every month when you get the bills, you say "not more bills to pay, we've never got anything left", this is affirming your intention to never have any money left. Your reality will keep matching this vivid expectation.

Consider how your emotion-charged thoughts, words, and deeds align... and what proportions of those are in the positive. Now think about a really upbeat person you know and how life mostly comes up daisies for him or her. It has been said, "there is no try, only do". Positive people do; they believe it will work, so there is no need to 'try'. Trying also implies there is no solid commitment.

Following this trilogy of purity in thought, word and deed, you will:

- **Eradicate all negativity.** Rid yourself of negative thoughts, as otherwise you'll soon be stopping yourself going forward. Stop hanging around negative people and listening to negative news. Use meditation to control your conscious thoughts.

- **Behave with integrity.** Many people say one thing and do another, but great leaders do not; they have congruence between what they think, say and do.

- **Be accountable.** Playing the blame game never helps; while we cannot control everything in our world, we can control how we respond. 'Being accountable' means that you take responsibility, and so you actually exert greater power over your results.

Summary.

If you follow your heart and have a pure intention, then that will win through in the end. When your thoughts, words, and deeds all align and you refuse to give in to temptation to take the easy way out... then you will prevail.

7. Character is Established through a Thousand Stumbles

We often don't give much thought to our own character. A combination of events, thoughts, and our own daily activities make an impression on the mind... thus creating our character as things happen.

Many of us look at negative events in our lives as "stuff that happens to us... bad luck", and fail to see the gap between this stimulus and our response. So busy are we in pinpointing who did this to us and how we deserve much more, that we then don't grow from the difficult experiences.

You have read of many hardships in each billionaire's early life, and Maha's was no different. It is from these early difficulties that people learn to face challenges head on. If you have had an easy life growing up, then you may not have established a robust character and you might overreact at your first business financial failure.

You may have surmised that from where we start in life does not make the difference; what makes the difference is our mindset and attitude. Do you believe that your abilities are fixed at birth? Or do you believe that genetics is just the start, and that you can grow and develop throughout your life?

When we are assessed at school, in sport, or in art, many times we take others' opinions on our abilities to heart... and for the rest of our life we say "I'm just not good at ....". But life is constantly dynamic and humans are built to adapt, change, and grow. Scientists have even found our brain cells (neurons) are able to regenerate upon stimulation after an accident. Nothing is fixed. Far from being "too old to change", with concerted development you can increase your magnetism and confidence at an older age.

If you believe that "character can be established through a thousand stumbles", then follow Maha's guidelines:

- **Believe it's a 'no' only until it's a 'yes'.** People often change their mind, sometimes completely. Laws change, relationships grow, so if your first proposal is turned down it does not mean that your every attempt will be met with no.

- **Fail forward.** Separating emotionally and learning from your mistakes, you will not allow failures to knock you backwards.
- **Don't compromise your beliefs.** People are inspired most by those who stand by their convictions. Always keep your promises, even those to yourself. Challenges maketh the man or woman, if you stand up for what you believe in the midst of that challenge.

Summary.

Knowing that you can change your outlook and even strengthen your character through life's events, gives you great power. Rather than letting obstacles or setbacks take you emotionally downward, you can learn from them and grow, always keeping to your own inner guideposts.

8. Everyone is Great in their own Place

This principle acknowledges the differences in individuals, and the leverage that seeking others with complementary strengths can provide.

A very positive, single-minded visionary like Maha works effectively with a detail-oriented, practical person like Bob, even though they have very different personalities. That said, they both have a stubbornness to get the job done and be successful, and both maintain a high integrity.

While many young entrepreneurs seek others just like themselves to partner with, even consciously turning away from practical, detailed personas, it's often more fruitful to find those with different aptitudes to our own. That way, a great company can be built from varied types of thinking and acting.

"Perfect partners don't exist. Perfect conditions exist for a limited time in which partnerships express themselves best." – Wayne Rooney

Identifying your personality type and using a framework to recognise others' core strengths can be a good first step to apply this principle as it allows greater understanding of our differences. The other elements that this principle suggests are:

- **Cultivate strong relationships.** No man or woman stands alone; each of us needs to interact to achieve our goals. If you are likeable, grateful, and flexible, you'll develop good relationships in business.

- **Match the task to the person's strengths.** Judging people's skills and personas quickly is crucial in finding the right person for a job. Once you have placed the right person in the right task and shared the objectives, allow them to get on with their job.

- **Expect people to do their best.** When you expect the best from others, they work harder to meet your stated belief in them. (As proven in various research studies). Focus on their strengths.

Summary.

"Everyone is great in their own place" is about finding others different to you when forming your team, those who provide strengths you don't have. The right personality type is supportive; the partner or worker will let you shine in your specialty too. "Your way is the best for you, but that is no sign it is the best for another"[34], says Maha.

9. Create your own Destiny

You might notice that among those in this book, none have ridden on the coattails of their parents. Maha and the Billionaires in this book have not followed the path set by our society, such as: attend further education, get a job, and buckle down to work. Each has believed he is the creator of his own destiny.

When you blame others for your situation, the world controls you. When you keep taking actions towards your chosen goal, then you control the world.

Although we are born with everything we need to make a success in this world, many of us are conditioned to believe that we lack something. You might think of children born without arms and so on, but look carefully... if there is disadvantage, there is always a corresponding ability or attitude that helps that individual overcome their adversity and, in doing so, inspire others.

Those without able bodies often overcome society's labels and seem happy as they are. But old labels like "poor, slow, stupid, fat, wimp, bad with money"—i.e. nothing permanent nor in most cases even true—stick to many of us quite able people, colouring our world and holding us back from a challenge.

Question any past labels and conditioned beliefs you notice, and start to realise that very little about you is permanent or pervasive.

Dreamers rule the world! To create your own destiny:

- **Foster self-belief.** Over time we may feel beaten down by others' envies, labels, and fears. Our mother may try to protect us and argue against our dream; our brother may try to put us down so he can feel stronger; but we alone must back ourselves. Take away the noose of racism, sexism, or poverty... and refuse to believe you are any less different and any less capable than others.

- **Think resourcefully**. Maybe there are few resources at your fingertips: little money, education, or powerful friends... but what can you tap? An optimist believes that the solution exists and it's only a matter of finding it. They think that setbacks are just temporary snags and a failure is an isolated case and not a reflection on themselves. This allows external resources to flow their way without any blockades.
- **Manage your own thoughts**. Your conditioned beliefs are keeping you from climbing the mountain. Listening to your inner voice of fear stops you from doing many different things that lead to contentment.

Your inner voice may even stop you from becoming fit and healthy. That's why personal trainers on *The Biggest Loser* show get contestants to tackle the scariest challenge they've ever done. Once you've taken action on something you thought impossible—and achieved it—you start to really believe you can do other things too, especially smaller things.

Another way to get over the fear of taking a new direction is to start taking small steps, grow in confidence, and remind yourself with new positive words where you are headed.

Summary.

"If I can do that, (walking a tightrope, bring up four children, etc), I can do anything." It's time to break off the shackles of your past conditioning, ignore any past labels, and move forward. To create your own destiny, get used to taking actions despite your fear and then back yourself. Expect more from friends or family in a positive way and they will rise to it.

10. All Power is Within You

"Life is full of opportunities, regardless of your origins or where you live." – Maha Sinnathamby

Believing this maxim means that finally you've given up the concept that success is built on luck, stars, good timing, magic, or inheritance. Nothing in life is easy or a matter of standing in the right place at the right time. The truth is—as Maha demonstrated when waves of challenge came—consistent effort, seeking solutions, and persistence is the only way to achieve your dreams.

You already may believe that we are all equal, no matter where one lives or how poor the surroundings. A start in life in poverty is difficult to overcome—but not impossible for those prepared to learn. Because Maha's parents believed strongly in personal development through education, Maha himself made it a tenet of his life, and ultimately this value inspired Springfield's 'Education City'. Springfield boasts one student for every three residents, the highest student/resident ratio in Australia.

Maha's inspiration draws from Vedanta. Vedanta is an ancient wisdom (based on ancient Hindu texts) where all beings are the same; all part of one connected, infinite whole. In this spiritual theory, there is no God outside of us that we need to be good for. As every one of us is divine, all power is within us. The Bible also says, "the Kingdom of God is within us".

Miracles sometimes occur when fighting for our life in hospital or when we're lost, so how does this happen? Think of the miracles as coming from the life force—in Vedanta it's called Brahman—through the recipient's soul.

In this wisdom, it's your thoughts, words and deeds that dictate what is created in your life, not luck or chance or a punishment for wrongdoing. If you don't consciously move your thoughts, words and deeds as a team towards your goal, then you'll find things often happening that you don't want. Just as war doesn't bring peace, hate or disdain for another doesn't bring you love; it is because we are all one and whatever we give out will be brought back to us.

If all power is within us, then men and women who achieve great deeds are no better equipped as a human being for the challenge than you are. The tenets of this principle are:

- **Find your own motivation**. No matter what creed or ethnicity you are, or where you draw your inspiration from, the main thing is that you are reading success stories and biographies, religious texts or other works to give you strength to live a better life. Not only that, you can use these stories to inspire you towards a worthy goal and to believe in yourself.

- **Stop to recharge**. Life is often busy and the pace is taxing on us both mentally and spiritually. If you arise early, you can enjoy the peace of the early morning and re-connect to you. Meditation allows you time to still the internal noise, turn off external noise, and just be present. If you're not great with the lotus position, then meditate while walking in the quiet or sitting on a chair.

- **Try for having 'no anger, no desire, no fear'**. This is about letting go of the expectancy for a certain outcome and aiming for an even temper. While you cannot just stop these emotions outright, realise that ego-driven desires in the end cause misery. It's easy get angry when things go awry. It takes strength to take a step back, remember that you're becoming attached to the outcome or to someone's expected behaviour... and this will prevent you from getting too angry.

"Desires are bound by the laws of success and failure. Desires must bring misery. The great secret of true success, of true happiness, is this: the person who asks for no return, the perfectly unselfish person, is the most successful."[34]
– Swami Vivekananda (disciple and writer of Vedanta texts)

Summary.

Being unattached to the outcome is a very difficult thing to do. Maha himself admits this goal is "a work in progress", and yet through stepping back from our expectations and desires, we will no longer waste energy wallowing in failure or blaming others. Only through connection to spirit will we find peace and inner strength, not from anything or anyone around us.

CONCLUSION

When training to become a 'visionary', you can choose to follow the ten principles that Maha sets out, or tread your own path. Whatever the case, we are fortunate to have access to such visionary mindsets, glimpsed in biographies or feature articles. I encourage you to learn more about these six billionaires or multi-millionaires, especially their traits and habits.

"The story of the entrepreneur... is the story of forward progress, of pursuing one's dreams and goals no matter how outlandish they seem to others. The entrepreneur, like the pioneer, pushes boundaries in search of what's new, what's next. Sometimes, he brings the whole society with him, rushing forward together into a next phase of our communal human life." [38]
– Sam Wyly, self-made US entrepreneur

The billionaires of Australia bring influence and diversity to our political arena. Two of them in particular are making waves. One is a think tank called 'Lowy Institute of International Policy', sponsored by Frank Lowy. Lowy Institute hosts (in Sydney) many of our political leaders or policy experts for important public lectures. And the other is Clive Palmer's new 'Palmer United Party', with three seats in the Senate as of the writing of this book.

It might be hard to see how a billionaire in power can remain unbiased when voting on legislature that affects their wealth. Yet at the same time, their voices represent economic growth and employment. The wealthiest miners, like Gina Rinehart and Clive Palmer, employ a lot of Australians and their projects can bring great prosperity to rural areas.

Other billionaires invested in retail, property or media have undoubtedly survived through the lean times of several economic cycles by planning well and operating efficiently. That's why you should listen to the voices of those who have experienced success and hard times, rather than the fear-mongering voices of news media.

Now we just need some more diverse wealth builders—like you and me—to bring greater diversity to ideas for the future of Australia.

References

Introduction

1 Sydney Morning Herald, 'Aussies the World's Richest People: Credit Suisse'. http://www.smh.com.au/business/the-economy/aussies-the-worlds-richest-people-credit-suisse-20131009. 19 October 2013.

2 CapGemini World Wealth Report 2013 (website). http://www.au.capgemini.com/thought-leadership/world-wealth-report-2013-from-capgemini-and-rbc-wealth-management.

Gerry Harvey

3 Herald Sun, 'Gerry Harvey suggests horse ownership is good for the character of a person'. 17 October 2013.

4 Kidman, Matthew and Feher, Alex, Master CEOs: Secrets of Australia's Leading CEOs. Ch.14. Wiley, 2008.

5 Woopidoo.com Quotes.

6 Kirby, John. Gerry Harvey: Business Secrets of Harvey Norman's Retailing Mastermind, Wiley & Sons, 2003.

7 Tracy, Brian. *The Psychology of Selling*, 2006.

Harry Triguboff

8 ABC 7.30 report. Harry Triguboff interview.

9 BRW Rich 200, May 2013, p.45-46

10 Meriton website. www.meriton.com.au/about-us/about-meriton/. Accessed October 2013 and February 2014.

11 Koch, David. *The Kochie Blog*. Accessed October 2013.

12 Australian Business Women's Network. 'Innovative Business a Shoe-In for Sascha Griffin'. http://www.abn.org.au/business-resources/innovative-business-sascha-griffin/. December 2008.

13 Lee Simonson, 'Diamonds in the Backyard'. Publisher, Heartwarmers.com

Frank Lowy

14 Margo, Jill. *"Frank Lowy: The Biography"*, 2000, HarperCollins Publishers.

15 Taylor, Brent D. *"The Outsider's Edge"*, John Wiley & Sons. 2007.

16 The Financial Review Smart Investor magazine, July 2013.

17 Business Review Weekly, *'Westfield sell-down: How the Lowys' fortune is going private'*, BRW.com.au, 1 March 2013.

18 Flemming, Jane. "Fast Track to Success", 2000, Penguin Books.

19 Universal Stars website. "19 Lessons Learned in Facing and Overcoming Challenges" www.universalstars.com.au/19lessons/. (Karen Corban).

20 Gome, Amanda, Smart Company, "Personal Development, Private Growth". www.smartcompany.com.au/growth/economy/4338-.html (Karen Corban).

21 Gilbert, S. J. Harvard Business School. 'Performance Persistence in Entrepreneurship' (paper), http://hbswk.hbs.edu/item/5941.html, 2008.

22 Koch, Richard, *"The Star Principle"*, 2010, Bolinda audiobook.

23 Colvin, Geoff, *"What it Takes to be Great"*, Fortune magazine (at money.cnn.com), 19 October 2006.

Clive Palmer

24 Sydney Morning Herald. *'Clive Palmer opens Palmersaurus dinosaur park at Coolum resort'*, www.smh.com.au, 14 December 2013.

25 Parnell, Sean. *"Clive: The Story of Clive Palmer"*, HarperCollins Publishers, 2013.

26 Sydney Morning Herald, *'Government approves Clive Palmer's Coalmine in Queensland'*, www.smh.com.au, 21 December 2013.

27 Koch, Richard, "The Star Principle", 2010, Bolinda audiobook.

Kerry Stokes

28 Egan, Colleen. Sunday Times Magazine, Kerry Stokes Interview in full. Read at PerthNow.com.au. 13 April 2008.

29 Wikipedia sources. http://en.wikipedia.org/wiki/GWN7

30 Knox, Malcolm. Sydney Morning Herald, *'Behind the Veil'*, SMH.com.au, 19 October 2013.

31 Seven Group website, http://www.sevengroup.com.au/our-investments/seven-west-media. Accessed November 2013.

32 BRW Rich200, p.34, May 2013.

33 Switzer, Peter. The Australian, *'Simply Brilliant'*. www.theaustralian.com.au, June 2011. (Gabby Leibovich quote).

34 Bannister, Brooke. ABC Perth, *'Who are you, Jack Bendat'*, http://www.abc.net.au/local/audio/2012/01/19/3411537.htm, 19 January 2012.

35 Greene, Robert. *"Mastery"*, 2012, The Penguin Group US.

Maha Sinnathamby

36 McCredie, Karen. *Stop Not Till the Goal is Reached"*, 2012, Wiley.

37 Thomson, James. SmartCompany, *'Rich Pickings: Maha Sinnathamby: The rise, fall and return of a property Rich Lister and his 10 rules for success'*. http://www.smartcompany.com.au/finance/wealth-management. 12 August 2012.

38 "1000 Dollars and an Idea" website. http://1000dollarsandanidea.com/AboutSamWyly.htm

From Broke to Billionaire

About Nhan Nguyen

Nhan Nguyen has founded a mentoring and property training company, called Advanced Property Strategies. Taking all that he has learned in property and deal-making, and showing others how to do it, is Nhan's driving passion.

While studying a Bachelor of Science, Nhan read *Rich Dad, Poor Dad* by Robert Kiyosaki, and from that moment his grades started to decline as his passion for property emerged. His biggest learning from the book was, "Don't work for money; have money work for you."

With his university degree behind him, Nhan took a role with a property education company, earning just $25,000 per annum. What he didn't receive in cash he received in education, learning how to do deals, qualify leads and look for opportunities. After one year, Nhan changed jobs to work for a different property development and marketing company that was moving over 80 properties a year. He learnt how to tie up opportunities with little money and on-sell the properties at a significant profit.

After three years as an employee and aged just 23, Nhan quit working for someone else and moved into full-time investing. He has now done more than 70 deals worth $20 million in total. In the past 24 months alone, he has done 29 property transactions using none of his own money.

Nhan is also the founder of Green Mint Property Group, focussing on Property Investment and Development.

www.ingramcontent.com/pod-product-compliance
Lightning Source LLC
Chambersburg PA
CBHW072101290426
44110CB00014B/1771